Conscience
in
todays
world

Edited by JEREMY HARRINGTON, O.F.M.

Nihil Obstat:
　　Rev. Claude Bettendorf, O.F.M., J.C.D.
　　Rev. John J. Jennings, S.T.D.

Imprimi potest:
　　Very Rev. Roger Huser, O.F.M.
　　Provincial

Imprimatur:
　　✠Paul F. Leibold
　　Archbishop of Cincinnati
　　June 17, 1970

Cover design by Lawrence Zink

SBN O-912228-01-6
Library of Congress Catalog Card Number: 72-132546
© 1970 St. Anthony Messenger Press
All rights reserved

Printed in the U.S.A.

Contents

Introduction

remember the days when most of us expected the Church to give us *the* answer on almost any issue from how to discipline our children to the historical facts of the Spanish Inquisition? Theologians gave us precise directives like the interpretations of the fasting laws: toast and coffee for breakfast, eight ounces for lunch, and 32 ounces as the norm for a full meal. You were excused, of course, if you were pregnant.

We were encouraged in those days "for peace of conscience" to check with Father on almost any decision "just to be sure." In the 50's, for example, couples were often advised to consult with Father before deciding to practice rhythm.

Now if you ask Father, he may well say, "Don't ask me. Form your own conscience!" Many of us haven't been very well prepared for this. Suddenly at a crucial moment in the game of life we've been thrown the ball. Some of us are not sure which way to run and we are afraid that we may fumble.

And it is a crucial moment in the game. Preachers try to stimulate our consciences to rid our world of racism, to help the poor in Appalachia and the dying children in Bombay. Our society has become so open as far as civil law goes, that one can do privately almost whatever he wants. Abortion is no longer against the law in several states. Nudity becomes more common in movies and stage plays. Dating restrictions on the part of society at large provide little moral protection. One-to-one dating from the eighth grade on is socially acceptable in many circles. Occasions of sin are regarded by some as a thing of the past. Many collegians find it hard to believe that there was once a 1 a.m. check-in time in girls' dorms even in state universities. Moral direction today has to come largely from one's own conscience.

All this makes parents very unsure of how to help form and guide the consciences of their children. Since their own childhood, student dissent, date-arranging computers, LSD and marijuana, SDS, the pill, sensitivity weekends, nuclear weapons and napalm have become a part of our complex world. We live in a time of transition, of rapid cultural change. For what shall we prepare our children? Is courtship with non-Catholics to be encouraged in an ecumenical age? Church attendance with Protestant friends? Has affluence done away with penance? Are parents who object to mini-skirts and to all nudity in movies being prudish?

We used to think that almost every case was

covered in the file of conscience. We just had to pull out the card and find the one-sentence solution.

But now we are continually confronted with new facts and insights from the knowledge explosion in psychology, medicine, biology, physics, anthropology, sociology, and new discoveries even in history and theology. The principles of morality are there, certainly, but the circumstances are always shifting and a little different in every situation. It is hard to say that anyone has *the* answer for everyone for all times.

Moreover, there has been a great shift in the material of conscience. Previously the emphasis was on strictly personal observance of the Commandments, with a heavy emphasis on the Sixth and Ninth: impure thoughts, sinful looks, telling or listening to obscene jokes, matters of fast and abstinence, Mass attendance and work on Sunday, respect for parents, honesty and truthfulness. Now the emphasis, especially among the young, has shifted to the problems of society: racism, the morality of war, poverty, overpopulation, pollution of our environment, the infringement on personal dignity by technology and business. Conscience has focused on the world, and it is a different and changing world.

To help bewildered parents in this turbulent world, Ethel Marbach shares her experiences as mother in "To Catch the Conscience of a Child." Parents are the artists dealing with the mystery of a person and the mystery of conscience.

Fr. Cyrin Maus seeks to cast light on the shadowy concept of conscience. It is the law within us, the focusing of the blurry "ought to be" into the sharper "I must" or "I may" or "I may not," a judgment of a past action. But most importantly conscience is "The Call of the Here-and-Now God." Conscience is the faith response of a believer made in cooperation with other believers who listen to the teaching authority of Christ voiced most obviously by the Pope.

Fr. Nicholas Lohkamp stresses that conscience must be seen in the framework of a response of love. We are not seeing how little we can do, but how we can best return love to our Father and our brothers and sisters. Conscience makes us able and eager to respond. We want to be creative about it, sincere, wholehearted. In the past some of us looked upon the Church and laws as taking away almost all necessity of our making personal decisions. So if there were no specific law, we thought we were "in free." We saw little reason to think for ourselves or decide for ourselves. We accepted what our parents and Father and Sister had thought out for us. Vatican II has made it clear that each of us must indeed use his own intelligence. The American Bishops likewise insisted in their annual statement in 1966: "No one is free to evade his personal responsibility by leaving it entirely to others to make moral judgments."

More recently the Bishops have reminded

that even in matters outside of ourselves and as far away from us as Vietnam, we have to make decisions. An 18-year-old, for example, must make up his conscience on whether he can actively participate in the war. To help all of us better understand conscientious objectors, Dr. Kenneth Eberhard discusses the principles according to which such a decision is made.

God Himself has ordained that each of us be allowed to freely make decisions. His attitude is reflected in the parable of the Prodigal Son. The father allows his son to leave him. He receives him back with love even though freedom has been abused by a sinful life. He knows that for many maturity comes only from unpleasant experiences. The baby learns to walk only after being left on his own with the risk of falling, protected of course from open stairs and broken glass.

The new stress on freedom is based on the assumption that mankind is growing up, is coming to age and is capable of responding to the values of life. It need not be precisely spelled out for adults what they can or cannot do in every situation. They should be able to accept the challenge: You are a Christian. Go live as one in every aspect of your life.

This is the way we're moving. Catholics are growing in moral responsibility. They are depending less and less on priests to settle specific conscience issues for them, and priests are less willing to do so.

This does not mean that laxity of conscience

is becoming widespread. Hopefully, dormant consciences are becoming active and operative. Each has to stand for and answer to the same Christ.

With so much depending on our conscience, the heightened interest in it is understandable. This book does not offer any tidy answers. It does offer challenging insights, expert analysis, practical advice.

We all are responsible for ourselves. Vatican II said, "Conscience is the most secret core and sanctuary of a man. There he is alone with God. . . ." At the same time we have to face reality. We are no more free to ignore reality in forming our conscience than in driving on an expressway. We each must choose our route to get to our goal, but we are not alone in going there.

—Jeremy Harrington, O.F.M.

Chapter I

Conscience:
The Call of God

Cyrin Maus, O.F.M., S.T.D.

If you ever want to stop the conversation at a
cocktail party, say something about conscience. Modern science hints at times that it
has rid mankind of this troublesome troll lurking
under the bridge of our awareness. But moral
consciousness is a live thing. Slice it up and it
still squirms. Cut off its tail and it grows a new
one.

We should know more about conscience, not
just as Christians but even as persons trying to
become more human. Let's ask first what conscience is not, then what it is, then how it is a
part of man's affair with God. In the next chapter, last part, we'll also speak in general about
forming our consciences, that is, how to "make
up our minds" about the right thing to do in
particular situations.

What Conscience is Not

I was still sleepy when I got in the car this morning. Sleepy plus absent-minded equals "crunch." I forgot all about the car next to me in the garage. It was brand new, but its fender crumpled like a Model T. I felt miserable.

Misery at ruining something new is not conscience. What I did was not morally wrong. And (theologically) Father Superior was ready to buy that. My "guilt" was real, though. It was a feeling a psychologist could explain as an echo from childhood, like from the times I knocked the lamp over or dropped the family's best platter. Parents have a way of letting you feel that some things are "no-no's." But that kind of feeling is not conscience.

The moral sense is not just our need for approval, whether from Mother, the boss or the Justice Department. It is not just our desire to excel or disappointment when we don't. Conscience is neither guilt, worry, dissatisfaction nor restlessness. For conscience is not just a *feeling*.

What Conscience Is

What it deals in is knowing and deciding. Briefly, it is a *person's* sense of right and wrong, his *awareness* of responsibility. It is there when a person realizes that he is answerable for what he does. He can recognize this both before he does something and afterwards.

Part of the problem is that we use "conscience" to point to no fewer than three states of mind, either separately or all mixed together in one. First, we sense what ought to be. Second, we realize we have to do something about it. Third, we look back and judge whether what we did was right or wrong.

A Sense of "Ought"

Vatican II uses the word in this sense: "In the depths of his *conscience*, man detects a law which he does not make for himself but which he has to obey" (*The Church in the Modern World*, 16). Here "conscience" almost stands for a person's "double," a "self" somehow alongside himself. Or perhaps better, a man's "innermost center" where he senses good or evil.

This "sense of what ought to be" may come over you at times all at once. But usually it's a kind of knowledge you get only gradually and perhaps never very clearly. It's a personal conviction without words. You "see" value without being able to put your finger too precisely on what you see.

To say this sense is not a feeling doesn't mean all feelings are absent. In fact, feelings help us recognize our awareness of what should be. Think of the dim sense of uneasiness you have when you're on your way to tell somebody off. Or the vague sadness or sense of "what's the use?" you try to hide when forbidden pleasure suggests itself. Or the subtle glow of expectation you feel when you hit on a way to show some-

3

one you love him.

Feelings like this help us identify that almost hidden reaching for value that grows in a back corner of our hearts. Over, in and behind almost everything in life, there it is—that unnameable consciousness of how things ought to be, which keeps us strangely uncomfortable with things the way they are.

A Sense of Responsibility Here and Now

What we just described, theologians prefer to call "moral consciousness." The word "conscience" they usually keep for what is here our second meaning.

Used in this sense "conscience" is operating when you state to yourself the dos and don'ts in a particular situation. You focus the blurry "ought to be" into a sharper "I may" or "I must' or "I must not." It's your practical judgment of what you have to do to make things what they should be. So it's your sense of your own responsibility regarding a concrete case.

Here conscience is quite *individual*. You can talk about someone else being your conscience, but eventually it is you who have to make up your own mind. Mother, the Pope, even Uncle Sam can help, but *I'm* the one finally responsible for what *I* do. I'm the one who decides.

Conscience is therefore also *specific*, not just general, or theoretical. To decide what he's to do about Vietnam, a young man can't just argue in theory about killing or about defending freedom. He has to decide here and now: can he responsibly allow *himself* to get involved in *this* war? Obviously, general principles have something to do with the decision. But "war" is not the same as "war in Vietnam for *me*."

It's clear also that our awareness of responsibility is part response. To decide is to reply to an actual situation. We come onto a set of circumstances, try to "read" them and then react to what we see in terms of who we are.

Thus, when *I* end up telling myself "Do this" or "Don't do that," it is like a bird flying. Conscience takes a direction which is partly the outcome of the way things are blowing. But the independent force of my own identity (like the thrust of the bird's wings) helps determine what I decide on. I bring to each situation the total disposition to good or evil which has been growing quietly in my heart. But what makes this moral sense definite is the case presented to me right here and right now.

Certain things follow from what we've discovered so far. First, conscience decisions are *subjective*. They depend on how *we* read situations. Also on the habitual dispositions *we* bring. In fact, it's possible to "follow your conscience" and still be dead wrong, in some cases even guilty.

The second consequence is also clear. Individual conscience is the final umpire determining whether what I do is morally acceptable or blameworthy. Traditional Catholic theology has always taught that an act is sinful only if I

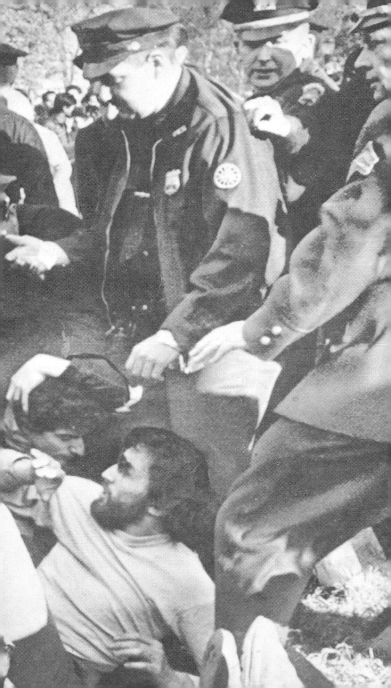

realize it and intend to do it anyway.

But this principle applies *only* where I have sufficiently "formed" my conscience, for I may read the situation incorrectly—because of negligence or because my habitual disposition may be blunted by the times I've kidded myself in the past. In this case, the simple fact that my conscience says something is all right does not guarantee that it is so.

For instance, we can fall into a habit of misjudging others because we are closed to any but our own point of view. We may have a system of values which glorifies working for a living. A value system like this can be accepted as an assumption which has never been examined. But on the basis of just such a presupposition, we can feel very justified in voting against new benefits for welfare recipients. The point is that many people might never *realize* that this may be wrong. Being unaware of guilt does not necessarily take away all guilt.

A Looking Back in Judgment

We've seen so far that conscience is both the indefinite sense of what ought to be and the determination of one's own responsibility in individual cases. Conscience is also the judgment a person makes of his own deeds once he has done them.

It is in this third sense that we use the word in expressions like "examination of conscience" and "there is nothing on my conscience." We speak of people with "guilty consciences" or of people who enjoy "peace of conscience."

Here again conscience is a matter of knowledge and not merely of feeling. Often we have to live through something before we can say we really know what it is all about. Marriage, for instance. So too the judgment that we make about the right and wrong of something before we do it must be tested after we go through with it.

Feelings certainly accompany this knowledge: the feeling of uneasiness and restlessness, sadness and depression at recognizing guilt, the quiet joy and satisfaction that can come only from an upright conscience. But feelings can be deceptive. Guilt feelings are not necessarily an abdication of moral guilt. And a sense of well-being is no absolute sign that we have nothing on our consciences. A truly good conscience will probably be one that leaves me a bit dissatisfied with what I have done, but not to the extent that I worry myself sick about it.

Conscience and Man's Affair with God

So "conscience" means a lot of things. But we haven't even mentioned what is most important. Our conscience is the main place where we carry on our lifelong dealings with God Himself.

All that goes on between God and man can be compared to a courtship. In revealing Himself to us, God woos us and we respond in faith

9

and hope. To see the precisely religious dimension of conscience, we must try to understand what "revelation" means and what is involved in our response.

Divine Revelation

For another person to know me, I have to let him in on who I am. I must open a window on my "me" or else we will remain like two ships that pass in the dark. If two people are ever going to fall in love, one of them has to give in and say something honest about himself. And, marvelously, this is usually all it takes to get something started. One's self-disclosure leads the other person to trust enough to reveal part of himself in return. In the process, both persons are "created" for each other and something wonderful begins to happen to them.

God makes love to us in much the same way. Slowly and quietly during our lives He lets us in on the huge, fascinating mystery of who He is. He does this in many ways but when suddenly we recognize *Him*, it always comes as something wonderfully unexpected. God reveals Himself to us and we are struck by the fact that we have not deserved His care for us. Caught up in the powerful pull of His self-disclosing concern for us, we are drawn to Him to be created even more fully.

Revelation is not so many facts. It is God letting us in on Himself. We grow vaguely aware that He is "for us." Oh sure, we can sometimes point to events in our lives or in the history of His people where we recognize His strange and powerful presence: a prayer is answered, some certain danger is miraculously avoided. For the most part, though, His presence is shadowy and unnameable at best. Even when He opens a window on Himself for us, we cannot define Him or find the magic charm that makes Him our ready genie. He remains like some deep, strongly unsettling, satisfying hope. He draws us out from where we are into the dark dim warmth of His far-off, present love.

God reveals Himself in a special way in Jesus. This calm, disturbing man lived and died in a distant land and time. He named the unnameable presence and spoke of Him as someone near and dear, in fact as "Father."

Jesus was a man who revealed what God is like. Little people suddenly felt themselves fall headlong into the pull of His person. His disciples really understood neither the power which drew them to Him nor the precise shape of the promises He made to them. They were confused when the religious leaders of that day had Him killed. But then they wakened to the meaning of everything when He stood in their midst as living Lord.

Jesus lives as the self-gift and promise of God even to this day. He is present like a spoken word in the beckoning mystery of human loving. His dying and rising still leads us to Him when we celebrate the sacraments of His Church. In a certain but symbolic way, the Church itself still presents to all mankind the Way, the Truth, the Life which He is as God for us.

Man's Faith

Revelation, then, is God giving Himself to us as presence and as promise. Divine revelation, like any self-disclosure, awakens trust and response in the one who becomes aware of it. This trusting response is what we call man's faith.

Faith begins with a recognition. We slowly wake up to God's presence and promise in our own experience. We begin to see the call to make a return commitment of ourselves to Him. The shape of this commitment dawns on our awareness gradually as the reality of God-revealing-Himself-to-us sharpens in focus.

We can refuse to believe, of course. Faith is a recognition, but no one is so blind as the person who refuses to see. Even when we have come to this initial insight, we can refuse to give in any further. Faith, true faith, takes place in an experience of trusting which can best be described as "melting" or "getting soft." It is like what happens between lovers. Husbands and wives sometimes have a kind of falling out. They get stubborn with each other so neither even understands the other's tentative gestures at making up. But, then, through some honest word of self-revelation, the miracle of trust is suddenly born again and both the stony stubbornness and lack of understanding melt away together. Faith, too, happens when we "give in"

to God. We decide to unbolt the door of our hearts to Him and all of a sudden we begin to understand him again.

Believing is also hoping. God's revelation is full of certain, but not always clear, promises. In giving in to Him, we embrace a meaning for ourselves which is future. God Himself, not yet altogether possessed, becomes the direction in which we take each new step.

Finally, just as God lets us in on Himself in a special way in Jesus and the Church, so also our believing is something we do together in the Body of Christ. When I believe God and commit myself to Him personally, I *am* Christ, I *am* the Church. We make the Church happen in us and thereby become something more than what we are in ourselves. We collect the response to God which all of creation, all men, groan toward from the depths of their being. We utter this response in our consenting "Amen" so full of hope. Our answering "Amen" *together* is the very sacrament which makes the end present and possible.

Questions for Discussion

1. What idea of conscience were you taught as a child? What is your concept of conscience now?

2. What three different states of mind do we describe by the word *conscience*?

3. Consider the hypothetical case of a three-year-old child abandoned on an island and living the rest of his life there without any human contact. Would he have a conscience?

4. Is it possible to sense something as wrong without being able to express exactly why it is wrong? How reliable is such a "feeling"?

5. In the strict sense, can someone else ever be your conscience?

6. What factors do you consider in judging the morality of a situation?

7. Is it true that every decision of conscience is a subjective decision?

8. Is it possible to follow your conscience and still be dead wrong? How?

9. Make up a case of someone deliberately forming his conscience wrongly.

10. Is it possible for a person to be unaware of guilt but still guilty?

11. Is it possible to have guilt feelings and still be free of any real guilt?

12. If Revelation is not just so many facts and truths, what is it?

Chapter II

The Conscience
Of a Believer

Cyrin Maus, O.F.M., S.T.D.

the general structure of the relationship between God and man is this: God reveals, mankind believes. The understanding of conscience which we outlined in the foregoing chapter fits nicely into this framework. We shall look again at conscience—as the sense of "ought," as the sense of responsibility in a particular circumstance and as the judging of our actions—against the background of revelation and faith.

God's Presence to Our Moral Consciousness

God is not dead. He is merely being Himself. He is no more hidden today than He ever was. It just seems so because for a while we had gotten very used to pointing to something about ourselves or even to the Church and saying, "There He is." When, finally, we realized that this wasn't God after all, we began to write His obituary. But make no mistake. God is very much alive. He is faithfully acting in His own way because that's the way He *is*.

If we look within ourselves with openness and the compliance of a lover, we can find Him right away. He is there in what we've called the undefined sense of what ought to be.

This "law which we do not make" is not God Himself. Like human persons, God speaks in words. The word I write is not *me*. And yet I am *in* my words just as my breath is still on and in my spoken words which fly out like kites to the persons I talk to. God speaks to us in our hearts and gradually, like children learning how to talk, we say back to ourselves what He speaks. What we repeat to ourselves is this "moral sense." It is not God Himself, but He is present in it and through it.

This sense of "oughtness" remains misty and indistinct. It also develops. It grows on the attitudes we take on at our mother's breast, in the daily give-and-take of the family circle, in the values and causes fought for in the society to which we belong. As God shows us Himself in these attitudes and relationships and values and causes, many questions rise up in our hearts. A great restless yearning begins to emerge in our consciousness.

To these questions and to this yearning, the special revelation given in Jesus and proclaimed by the Church comes as truly good news for the man softened up for trust and love.

The vague moral sense sharpens into the image of Jesus' loving response to His Father. The pattern of His behavior—the full unknowing submission to His Father which leads beyond the cross and death to resurrection—shows the shape into which our moral sense is carving us. Jesus' full gift of Himself to others brings to sharper definition what we, His followers, are being summoned to: the reconciliation of everything in a way we by ourselves could never bring about.

Revelation and Faith in Our Sense of Present Responsibility

The second meaning of "conscience" described above—our focused sense of responsibility here and now—relates closely to the sharper definition of the moral sense which appears in the revelation of God which we find in a special way in the life of Jesus and His Church.

When I am brought face to face with a concrete situation—for example, whether to pay my income tax or not, whether to be drafted or to be a conscientious objector—I find a need to decide specifically "Do this" and "Don't do that." I have to take responsibility and I have the freedom to do so, but I am not a law unto myself. What I am, the situation and God's revelation are all involved in my decision.

What I am and have come to be meets and responds to what I read in the situation before me. The meaning of this situation is somehow clarified by God's revelation, particularly by that special revelation made in the person and life of Jesus and treasured by His Church. My response must somehow, therefore, be a faith response.

"What I Am and Have Come to Be"

Most of us have probably absorbed to a greater or lesser extent the Church's way of looking at life, which is at least in part a product of supernatural revelation. The "law which we do not make" has taken particular form in our minds by reason of our knowledge of the Ten Commandments and of what Jesus stood for and spoke of in the Gospel.

But we are also products of many other factors—our abilities, our temperaments, our likes and dislikes, our interest patterns, the momentum to good or evil established by the sinfulness or ready responsiveness of our past lives.

Likewise, without our realizing it, we tend to think very much like the other people in our culture. The news media, advertisers, national propaganda machines, the people we associate with have all influenced us. We have a set of values—things we want to happen. What makes something a *value*—for instance, possessions or democracy—is not necessarily that they are good in themselves. Something is really a value merely if a group of people hold it to be desirable. (Social philosophers thus speak of values as "operational structures of a society.")

The point here is that I bring all these

things to every situation I face. They are all part of what I am and have come to be. Revelation, our relationship with God, has certainly had a hand in making us what we are. But so have many other factors.

Reading the Situation in the Light of Revelation

What he is and has come to be has a lot to do with the way a person who is more or less truly a Christian reads a live situation which demands a decision from him. But because he cannot trust himself implicitly, he must try to see the full meaning of each situation. Part of the meaning is the *revelation* in it.

Situations don't talk, just as black ink on a printed page doesn't talk. In both cases, they are "words." Their meanings are what is intended by the one who speaks them and understood by someone else.

In a situation where a definite act is required of the Christian, the Author of the "Word" is God Himself. He is not a God "out there" someplace, but He is a here-and-now God. Everything we see and do as human beings is something personal between Him and us.

His meaning is not always so clear. He speaks somewhat like a modern poet whose words require study to be understood. We have to look not just at this one little verse in His writings—the present situation—but also at the whole poem He is writing us in the various circumstances of our life.

That too doesn't clear up the words completely. We must look further to the masterpiece which has come from His pen, the Gospel of Jesus. Also to the way it has been sung again and again down through the centuries around the Easter fires and Eucharistic tables of His followers. In other words, in reading the meaning of the present situation, God's revelation and the Church's teaching can help.

Even after all this, however, there is still some doubt remaining. The 18-year-old Christian cannot find any reference either in the Gospel or in the Church's teaching about *him* and *this* war in Vietnam. Jesus' statement about "turning the other cheek" certainly says something to the present situation. But what about the other thing about "laying down your life" for another human being? So reading the situation may have *clarified* things a bit, at least to the extent that he can see a number of new dimensions to it. Nevertheless, his effort at seeing the meaning of God's call right here and right now has not dictated precisely what he should do or not do. *He* must still decide.

Our Response as the Reply of Faith

The Christian must come to a specific decision in a response which is both free and of faith.

His response is free because he is a human person. If he is at one with God, his freedom is strengthened by the Indwelling Spirit of God. For this reason, his decisions can be deliberate acts of his own and not just the result of massive forces outside him that toss him along like driftwood on a rip tide. Of course, his decisions are always responses to conditions around him. But he determines himself. His free will is like a surfer's balanced control over his board—it sets the line he ends up following not on its own, but by using the forces moving in the wave of present circumstances. Thus we feel responsibility in making decisions precisely because we are able to respond with a will of our own.

The Christian's response must be a faith response. If he merely lets himself be caught up in the current of public opinion, he is not acting from faith. St. Paul has something unsettling to say to this: "All that is not from faith is sin" (Rom. 14,23). Our 18-year-old draftee must not just do what Spiro Agnew or Eric Sevareid says—or even Abbie Hoffman. If he is Christian, he must make a faith decision.

This kind of faith is scary. Inevitably, even when we possess the bold certainty of true faith, we are taking a chance. We pray "Thy will be done" not so much by God "in heaven" but here "on earth"—by us. And the very fact we have to pray for this shows that we never avoid the risks deciding requires.

We take the awful risks that faith necessitates partly because we do believe and hope even against our doubts that God is "our Father in heaven." In doing this, however, we put our

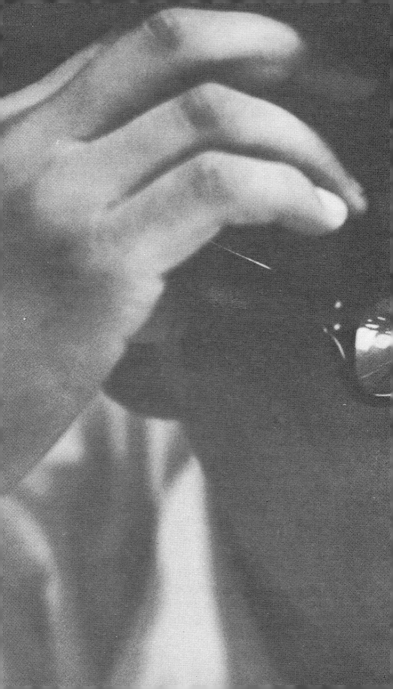

"The question I must grapple with at every moment and in every situation is: What is God's will for me in this unique situation? What would He have me do?"

very selves into our actions. A faith decision thus becomes a matter of presenting ourselves to God in the deed. What we do takes on a meaning which is not only what the act might mean in itself, but also what we intend. Faith is a personal response, the lovers' signs mean something to one another even though outsiders might see quite a different significance.

Some of the sense of being all alone in deciding can be avoided. The faith response is one we make with others, simply because it is faith. If we can sense in what we decide a harmony with what Jesus and the Church stands for, we have as much security as a man can have in this life. It is not a security which lights up all the dark places of doubt, of course. Faith is faith partly because it involves what the mystics call the "cloud of unknowing."

Nevertheless we still have Jesus' assurance: "Where two or three are gathered together in my name"—for instance, by agreeing on a concrete moral decision arrived at in faith—"there am I in the midst of them." It is no doubt because of His presence in the gathered believing of His followers that He tells His disciples in another place, "He who hears you hears me." It really helps the young conscientious objector to see the Fathers Berrigan at his side in a peace march. It really helps the soldier in Vietnam to have his chaplain boost his courage. The wonder of the two cases is that, although seemingly contradictory (and who can say which person made the "right" decision?), they both can be expressions of the same, identical faith. The Spirit breathes where He wants to and is not tied down by laws of human logic.

A Preview of Final Judgment

In the development of our theme of conscience as the voice of a here-and-now God, we have seen that He is present both in our sense of what ought to be and in our sense of a present responsibility. We must also identify His presence in the third state of mind we call conscience —the judgment we make on our deeds once we understand better what we meant by doing them.

God's presence to men as far as we are concerned happens in stages—in man's experience of nature, in his experience of history, particularly the history of Jesus and His Church, and in each man's experience of his own personal history that has brought him up to a responsibility here and now. From God's point of view, however, the various stages of His presence to men are all the same. If He is there, He is there personally in love, in summons and in judgment. His love is an outgoing gift of Self to us, His summons calls us out from ourselves in response, and His judgment takes all-seeing note of the truth or lack of our response. Our final judgment either as a race or individually is but our own eventual recognition of the truth of God's constant presence to us and of ours to Him. Recognition of truth takes note also of blame and worth.

Thus, the judgment we make of ourselves in looking back on what we have done is a presentiment of the divine judgment we shall come to anon. It is already a view from God's eternal vantage point because what we have done is done forever now. It is a participation too in His presence to us—we are present to ourselves in the consciousness we have of ourselves as good or evil or a mixture of both. His presence calls us on, as indeed the judgment we make of ourselves calls us out to respond more fully while there is still time to be present to.

In all of conscience, therefore, we must recognize the presence of the Lord. His voice is the one that counts, not our own voice reassuring ourselves or the disapproving voice of our fellowmen. St. Paul says it very well:

"With me it matters very little that you or any 'Day of Man' pass judgment on me. I do not even pass judgment on myself. I have nothing on my conscience; but that does not mean that I have been acquitted. It is the Lord who passes judgment on me. . . . He will bring to light what is hidden in darkness and will manifest the intentions of men's hearts" (1 Cor. 4,3-5).

Questions for Discussion

1. How much do the teachings of the Church influence your decisions of conscience?
2. How much do you think TV has influenced your conscience? On what specific issues?
3. What does the author mean by the "revelation" that can be found in a situation? Can you think of any examples of this happening in your life?
4. "If a Christian lets himself be caught up in the current of public opinion, he is not acting from faith," the author says. Can you think of any issues today on which public opinion might be judged to run contrary to faith?
5. As far as making up our consciences on particular issues, what is the benefit of belonging to the Church?
6. Discuss the significance of this statement: "Our final judgment either as a race or individually is but our own eventual recognition of the truth of God's constant presence to us and of ours to Him."

Chapter III

Conscience
Equals
Response-Ability

Nicholas Lohkamp, O.F.M., S.T.D.

"Let's go to a movie!" you suggest to a group. Two people frown and the rest remain silent. The response was unfavorable. You drop the idea.

Mrs. Meyer is elected by the women's society as director of adult education. She takes hold and organizes a library of books and tapes, engages noted speakers, sets up special discussion groups on the new catechetical methods, creative retirement, business ethics and conscientious objection. She responded to the challenge. Her predecessor did not get beyond thinking what might be done.

A teacher senses quickly how well a class is responding. A comedian knows whether the audience is really "with him" or not. We readily perceive the response of others to us. In spite of our friendliness, Joe remains cool and distant. Tom warms up and flashes back interest. Our friendship deepens.

Conscience is response. It enables us to respond to God, to people, to situations. First of all, and most of all, we respond to God. Everything starts with the tremendous fact that God has acted first. St. John concisely reminds us: "In this is the love, not that we have loved God, but that He has first loved us" (1 John 4, 10).

God has loved us first and continues to love us without interruption. Everything that we do ought to be a response, an answering, a returning of that love.

Conscience is our ability to respond as free human beings capable of love. It is more; it is that in us which demands that we respond.

Conscience seen as *response-ability* gives us an active, creative role. Being conscientious is not merely doing what we are told to do, what is spelled out for us; rather it is dreaming up ways of pleasing, of returning love, of giving worthy gifts to someone who loves us very much and never ceases to do good things for us.

The Christian code is best described as a morality of responsibility. Vatican II has summed up nicely the current situation and thinking: "Throughout the world there is a similar growth in the combined sense of independence and responsibility. Such a development is of paramount importance for the spiritual and moral maturity of the human race. . . . We are witnesses of the birth of a new humanism, one in which man is defined first of all by his responsibility toward his brothers and toward history" (*Constitution on the Church in the Modern World* #55).

On this same idea of responsibility, one of the greatest moral theologians of our age, Fr. Bernard Häring, bases his teaching. He calls for a "full and living response" to God. To make such a return to God, man must take his tasks here on earth seriously and earnestly. Häring says, "We understand Christian morality as responsibility in the sense that the Christian in his relationships to himself, to his fellow humans, to the world of creatures, perceives a word and message which ultimately comes from God. This responsibility further requires that in his thinking, speaking and acting, in his personal relationships, and in his shaping the world he give a fitting reply, that he act responsibly and so much so that everything in the last analysis becomes a reply, a response that is worthy to be offered to God. . . ."

Thus for Häring and for such other giants of moral theology as Dietrich Bonhoeffer, H. R. Niebuhr and Robert Johann, responsibility is the basic principle and the unifying concept of morality. You shall respond to the Lord, your God, and to your fellowmen and to the needs and challenges of your world. Responsibility draws together all the various elements of ethical teachings. The most basic moral imperative challenges: be responsible.

And it is the *whole* person who makes this loving response. Conscience is not merely feeling, but neither is it merely a judgment by the

33

mind. Nor is it merely a raw act of the will deciding between good and evil. The whole person is engaged in an act of conscience. The whole person's capacity to respond to the good (ultimately to The Good, God) is expressed and made actual in a particular act here and now. I is *I* who evaluate, judge, decide, act.

So, conscience is not some little voice in me that is not me. Conscience is not a moral computer buried in my heart. Conscience is not some mental file cabinet which I can open and find "answers."

Conscience is my capacity to read my situation in the light of faith and to decide how I ought to act to be responsible. It is *I* who engage myself in a particular form of response in a particular situation to a particular value. Presupposing I am a believer, my response is my reply of faith to God. My response is my answer to God's call as I am able to hear it here and now and find myself able and obliged to respond so as to be faithful.

I Can Make Decisions

It is no use talking about conscience, however, unless we are agreed from the beginning that I really can make some choices. If I am not free, if I cannot control what I do or say, then I cannot be held accountable, I do not have the ability to respond.

We may sometimes feel anything but free when our obligations press in on us. We feel

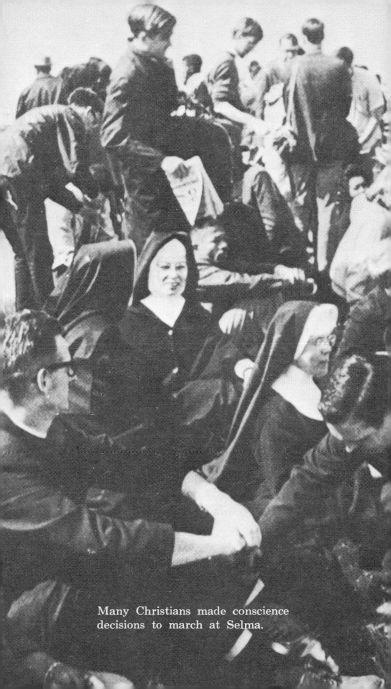

Many Christians made conscience
decisions to march at Selma.

"caught" by the needs of others (spouse, children, neighbor, community, parish), or forced by the heavy hand of authority. Indeed, to a greater or lesser degree, we are restricted.

But freedom is not an either/or matter. We do not have to be 100 per cent free or not free at all. If in a particular case we are only 20 per cent free, we are only 20 per cent accountable. Admittedly, forces outside us or within us can diminish our freedom or possibly take it away completely.

If someone drops LSD in our drink without our knowing it, while under the power of the drug we may not be able to act freely at all. During World War II prisoners in concentration camps were *forced* to do many things. But even in these extreme circumstances, as Dr. Viktor Frankl, who endured the hell himself, insists, the prisoners had "the last of human freedoms"— the ability to "choose one's attitude in a given set of circumstances." A man could allow himself to become so discouraged that he succumbed to despair, or he could nourish his indomitable spirit and continue to hope. Similarly, the person dying of cancer still has the ultimate freedom of choosing his response. He can love or hope or despair.

Our freedom can be lessened by moral forces as well as physical. If one student is causing the whole class to be punished, the rest of the students can put moral pressure on the offender to change. But the individual can withstand group pressure. In spite of the pressures that a college boy may feel from his friends and environment, he can practice chastity and refrain from premarital sex. An unmarried girl who becomes pregnant may be greatly pressured to have an abortion. But she can withstand the advice of her friends.

Our own emotions and drives can lessen our freedom. Fear or anxiety can make us more or less incapable of assisting a person in danger. We can become so angry that we really do not know what we are saying or doing. "I lost control of myself," we say. Sexual passion or strong feelings of disgust can and do influence us and diminish our freedom. When we are caught up in these emotions, especially when they are strong, we don't think clearly; we lose balance and perspective; we are less free, and so less responsible.

We should, of course, be aware that we can, by dwelling on certain thoughts and memories, by entering certain situations, willfully arouse our feelings and emotions. In such cases we are responsible and accountable for our diminished freedom. Thus, the man who deliberately stirs himself into a rage is responsible for any evil he foresees may result.

To the extent we are free, to that extent we are responsible. Most of us do not need to be convinced that ordinarily we are in charge of ourselves, and that we are indeed able to make decisions for good or for ill. That's one aspect of conscience.

Of course, freedom does not mean that we

are without restraint from any man or thing. Our decisions always involve us as persons and accordingly in relationship to other persons, our family, our neighbors, community, Church and God. Their welfare dictates how I exercise my freedom. My responsible decisions depend on much more than just my own personal preferences.

Conscience Demands Decisions

Living as a mature adult means all kinds of decisions—choosing Cheerios or eggs for breakfast, forgiving or harboring a grudge, going to Sunday Mass or not, accepting a bribe or not. No matter who we are, no matter what the situation, a human moral response necessarily involves us in decisions.

Even when a principle or law is involved? Certainly. In the past some Catholics saw a law as taking away the necessity of making a choice. "The law is clear; the law says. . . . Therefore, there is nothing for me to do but obey. There is nothing for me to decide."

Such an attitude is clearly "legalistic." It greatly oversimplifies reality. Obviously, we ought to listen and really try to understand all human and divine laws and most especially try to grasp the values to be fostered and protected by such laws. But I am still faced with the responsibility of judging, evaluating and acting. I must decide how and to what extent I am able to realize this law or teaching in my concrete activity. Moreover, any law, any teaching of the Church, is always *general*. No law, no teaching, can ever fully take into account the particular circumstances and concrete situations of individual persons. What is more, laws are always concerned with but one value at a time. Laws do not pretend to give any final solution to possible relationships of different values, or the conflict of values that may occur in concrete situations. Laws single out a certain kind of human activity and indicate something about its morality, e.g., murder is wrong; robbery is wrong; you must tell the truth; you must go to Mass on Sunday; you must not use the pill for contraceptive purposes.

Ordinarily, it may be quite simple to decide how to embody the particular value of a law in my life. I speak truthfully; I go to Mass; I do not use the pill. But it is not always so simple; sometimes it is exceedingly complicated. There are times when I would like to go to Mass, but mother is sick. I would prefer not to use the pill, but my non-Catholic husband insists and my doctor warns me not to get pregnant. I am caught in a tangled web of conflicting circumstances and values. Now what am I to do? One law says: go to Mass. At the same time another law says: honor and take care of your mother.

One teaching says: love your husband. Another says: care for and educate your children. Another says: do not expose yourself or others to serious danger of sinning. Another says: don't have children you cannot take care of. Another

"No matter who we are, no matter what the situation, a human moral response necessarily involves us in decisions."

says: don't use the pill. What am I to do? I *have* to decide!

I obviously cannot in this specific situation observe all the laws or follow all the teachings of the Church. So I have no choice but to choose. I must evaluate as best I can, and freely decide to do what I believe is the most responsible thing for me here and now.

Notice, what we are saying here in no way denies the existence of "absolute" laws, that is, laws which admit of *no* exceptions, e.g., the direct killing of innocent persons is always forbidden. Such a law would still only indicate what a person may *not* do with regard to one specific value. It does not indicate what a person *should do*, e.g., when there is question of saving the life of the mother or the child if both cannot be saved. Nor do such laws provide the answer to the problems which arise from the existence of evil, conflict of values, or relationship of values that can seriously complicate a concrete situation. Decisions must still be made in the concrete.

Often it might be easier for me to push the decision off on someone else. We can get advice and perhaps may be obliged to seek advice, but finally regarding my life *I* have to decide. As the American Bishops said at their meeting in November of 1966, "No one is free to evade his personal responsibility by leaving it entirely to others to make moral judgment."

We make decisions on two different levels: regarding particularly concrete actions (Shall I go to bed or watch TV?), and the level of basic options or choices which determine the whole direction of our lives (Do I live for myself or for others?). I can decide in a way that disposes of my whole self, gives direction to my whole life. Such a basic option or choice involves my fundamental relationship to God—for Him or against Him (mortal sin in the fullest sense). On the other hand, I make choices and decisions which concern this or that particular concrete action. Normally, a person will endeavor to make particular choices according to his basic option.

Much is left unsaid here, but the main point should be clear: conscience is the capacity and duty to be responsible, and that means ceaseless involvement in decision-making.

In the first form of the penance service at Mass, we accept responsibility for what we have done and what we *have failed to do*. Many times, as Harvey Cox has noted, "not to decide *is* to decide." Often the easiest course is to back off from a decision, to act as if the problem or challenge were not there. The typical mortal sin, as Monsignor Paul Hanly Furfey has noted, is the sin of noninvolvement. The sinner remains passive, living his own self-centered life. He avoids making a decision to help the needy around him. "I was hungry and you gave me no food; I was thirsty and you gave me no drink; I was a stranger and you did not take me in; naked, and you did not clothe me; sick, and in prison, and you did not visit me. . . ."

Our Conscience Must Be Formed and Informed

Facing reality means all of reality. The greatest reality for the Christian is God's love for us. This love has expressed itself in the revelation of the Old Testament and the Commandments given to God's people on Mt. Sinai. Above all, this love was expressed in God sending His own Son, Jesus, who taught us by word and example how to believe and love and live. We must be informed of what Jesus has told us.

He continues to reveal Himself to us directly through prayer, and also through the wisdom and advice of others. We can read His will in events and circumstances.

Before we can make a decision of conscience, we need "in-put." As Fr. Richard A. McCormick, S.J., stresses, "We are not free in the *formation of conscience* anymore than we are free to decide whether the world is flat or round." We seek relevant information from religious sources. We also have to search out and consider pertinent data from psychology, sociology, medicine, etc. We need insight into the values we seek and how to realize these values here and now in this activity. Often we'll need the advice of others. Our decisions must be as enlightened as reasonably possible. Conscience must be based on knowledge, not ignorance.

Business speaks of making a 360-degree decision, that is, of studying the entire context, trying to identify *all* the factors. If I am switching lanes on the expressway and miss seeing the car passing me on the left, I crash into it. I missed one of the factors. The engaged couple who have rationalized that they may anticipate marital rights may easily overlook the rights of a child that may be born of their intercourse, or the damage done to their own self-esteem or to the community.

We cannot think only of how well our brand of detergent cleans the dirt from our clothes. We also have to think of the effect the chemical agents contained in the detergent will have on our streams and rivers. The stress on cleaning up our polluted environment makes us aware of how completely interrelated our actions are. This is true in all aspects of our lives. We have to try to foresee all the consequences of our actions.

Love Promotes Creativity

Perhaps in the past the most neglected characteristic of conscience was its need to be *creative*. Too long have we expected the Church and priests, the state and lawmakers to tell us exactly what we have to do. If we did all that we were told to do, then we felt justified. If I went to Mass on Sunday, abstained from meat on Friday, fasted during Lent, and lived up to the Church's laws on marriage, I was a good Catholic. Such an outlook fosters resting content after the bare minimum is done. It is like a husband asking his wife: "How much do I have to love you? Exactly what things must I do?"

"The Christian must respond to the Lord, to his fellowmen, and to the needs and challenges of his world."

God has loved us first. Conscience urges us to generous response. Conscientious decisions arise from within a person; they are my free determination of myself as to how I am going to act here and now in response to God as I hear His call in this particular situation. How am I going to build up the self-confidence of my child? How am I going to give hope to my father who feels so defeated and shaken by the changes in the Mass? What can I do to bring about a fairer distribution of this world's goods and opportunities? What can I contribute to the battle for a cleaner environment? How can I foster real community in my parish?

In each decision and choice I am fashioning, building, creating myself in relation to the world, to other people, and most especially to God. With each new decision I change; I am no longer quite the same. With each new decision I grow, I become a better or worse person, a better or a worse Christian.

When we speak of conscience as making decisions that are free and creative, many become frightened. "What about God and His will?" they ask. "Doesn't conscience simply mean doing what is commanded, avoiding what is forbidden, and for the rest doing what I please?"

Of course, my decisions must be directed to doing God's will. But the question I must grapple with at every moment and in every situation is: What is God's will for me in this unique situation? What would He have me do?

There are laws, there are guidelines, there

are the general teachings of the Church, there are the deeds and words of Jesus in the Gospel. But, to my knowledge, there is not—nor could there be—a predesigned and concretely detailed plan that indicates to me in all the changing and varied situations of my life precisely how I am to act at any given moment.

God's will is that I freely and with love respond to Him, to my fellowman and to the situation. There are many ways in which God speaks to me: laws, teachings of the Church, world and human events, theologians, other persons, and especially through the Indwelling Spirit. But God expects me in freedom to *search* for His will, to search for what is right and good, to search for the course that will further human and Christian values. This is God's will for me. This is what characterizes the attitude of the creative person; this is what guides and motivates the creative person in what he decides to do, or not to do. How else can we be responsible?

Conscience Demands Sincere Decisions

Looking squarely at the complexity of the situation and viewing honestly God's and the Church's laws and the values at stake, is not easy. Sincerity is often difficult. Someone has defined man as the animal capable of endless self-deception. We can kid ourselves, rationalize our position, make excuses, tell ourselves that we are not strong enough to do what we know we ought. "The formation of conscience can easily become a monologue with ourselves," says Fr. McCormick, "rather than a dialogue with God." But if we are insincere, we are the only ones fooled. St. John in his first letter assures us that "God is greater than our hearts and all is known to him" (I John 3:21).

Sincerity means we seek to make our choices and decisions in the light of the Gospel, in light of the teachings of the Church, in light of the laws and wisdom of men. Sincerity means we want to achieve in our lives and our activity the greatest good for others. Sincerity means we really are aware of our sinfulness, our inclination to selfishness and idolatry, yet ever seek to repent and convert. Sincerity means we really want to grow and respond more wholesomely to others and to God in our lives and in our actions.

It is crucial that such a sincerity move us in all our decisions. To the extent that we are sincere we will be actualizing *genuine Christian consciences: our capacity—and obligation— freely, personally, creatively to respond to God by fulfilling our task here on earth in the human community.*

Conscience, then, is our capacity to live responsibly. What this means is well summarized in the book, *Responsibility in Modern Religious Ethics*, by Albert R. Jonsen, S.J.:

"Thus the responsible man as decision-maker is one who, while he admits that in great part established principle and rule suffice to order

life, is aware that the values which he accepts must be realized in new situations, amid new difficulties, with renewed energy and resourcefulness. He knows that he must continually endeavor to draw out of his personal and communal experience a new appreciation of the values. But he is also aware that his experience is unfinished and often deceptive. He attains new insights into his own reality and achieves new expression of those insights, but always by experiment, risk, trial and error. His moral creativity is more that of the apprentice than of the master: his strokes are tentative and often need to be retouched."

Some may ask: "Aren't these free and creative decisions of conscience pretty risky? Aren't the chances of error pretty great?"

Some conscientious decisions are simple, especially the less serious ones. We make them with moral certainty. We have little fear of being wrong. But many of our more serious decisions do involve risk. Should I change jobs or not? Should we have another child? Can I participate in this business venture?

Sometimes we are painfully aware of risk. The values involved may appear to be in conflict, the consequences may be unclear or uncertain, the authorities we consult may not agree. Yet we can no longer postpone decision. If we would wait for the clear light of certainty, we would fail to be responsible.

In such cases we prayerfully make the best choice we can in the light of our information

Our Christian responsibility
calls for day-to-day decisions
in response to the
world around us.

and our evaluation of the situation. We have the consolation of the guidance of the Holy Spirit. We know that God is our loving Father. He sees our intention and our good will. He will never blame us for a decision we have made in good faith. He appreciates the love that we are trying to give even through our stumblings. After all, conscience only makes sense when it is seen as a response to a God who *loves* us.

Questions for Discussion

1. What do we mean by minimalism in moral matters? What do we mean by legalism? Name some examples of minimalism or legalism as regards our obligation of attending Sunday Mass. Regarding fasting.

2. In what way has there been a growth of independence and responsibility in our world today?

3. Why is greater independence and responsibility necessary for the maturity of the human race?

4. In what way are we "responsible toward history." Give examples of how we might exercise such responsibility.

5. Discuss specific cases in which a person's freedom might be limited.

6. What freedom does a person dying of leukemia have left?

7. We speak of mob psychology being operative in a crowd. Could this limit human freedom? Take it away completely?

8. If in anger or passion we "lose control of ourselves," are we culpable? How would the degree of responsibility be judged? What if one foresaw that he might be "carried away" in a situation?

9. Give examples of possible conflicts of values.

10. What do we mean by our "basic option" in life?

11. In what way must conscience be creative?

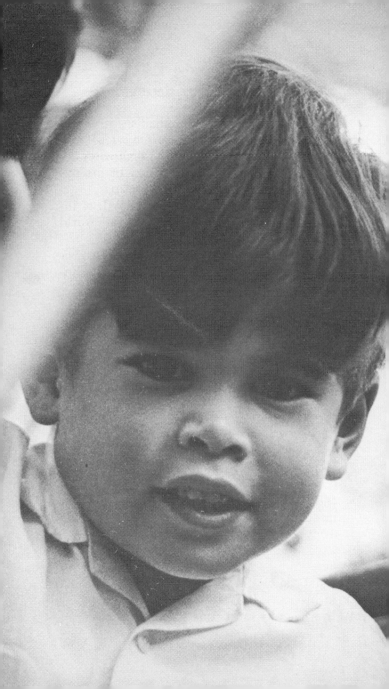

Chapter IV

To Catch
the Conscience
Of a Child

Ethel Marbach

are there any of us parents who do not wonder in weary moments if we are honestly doing enough, and doing that correctly, to give our children values that will stick and a conscience which will guide them safely in a turbulent world?

It is a difficult and endless responsibility, this molding of the young to Christian standards. We can take a hint from Shakespeare's cleverness. In *Hamlet* he used the theatrical device of a play-within-a-play "to catch the conscience of a king." The king was Hamlet's uncle, who, after murdering Hamlet's father (the former king), proceeded to marry Hamlet's mother—a string of actions which presumably were not conducive to his sleeping well. In watching the supposedly innocent diversion of the players, the king is cut to the quick by seeing them reenact the evil he has done.

The analogy to our "catching the conscience" of a child is as slight as a nylon thread but just as strong. We parents are the traveling players who must put on a good show for the instruction of our offspring. We are not out to shock them, as Hamlet's group did the king; nor are they murderers who must be brought to justice. They are reflectors. From our performance as conscientious parents, they will absorb and mirror as adults what they see on stage now. It is up to our creative craftsmanship to present an image which will be reflected for generations to come.

But before we can talk about forming the conscience of the young child, we must first be certain of the condition of our own consciences. We cannot give what we don't have. When first married, we don't have too much to give in the way of wise and impeccable example; we are too busy in the giving and discovering of each other. But then, no one expects mature judgments from the young couple just on their way with their first child. The patience, the ability to cope, and the wisdom to sort out the false from the necessary come only with experience. Even without maturity, however, parents must have a conscience which will not fail them. And this in turn relates back to *their* parents.

It must have such firm roots that it spreads and permeates all their actions, goals, tastes, talents and sacrifices. Conscience is not a push-button gimmick, a red and green traffic light that blinks Go and Stop. It is an attitude which possesses the entire being—the way you dress, write a letter, spank a child, treat your spouse, help a stranger like a Samaritan, share a pizza, mend and patch torn jackets, weed carrots and pick blackberries.

It wanders over from the negative field of sin to the positive ones of social conduct, involvement with nature and the arts, and work in the community. It will needle the musician who fingers a passage sloppily, the writer who writes carelessly and leaves it to the editors to fix, the teacher who does a better "snow" job than his pupils.

A person with a right conscience will act in the best interests of those beneath and above him and of those for whom and to whom he is responsible. Imagine, if there were more men of good moral conscience in the world of, say, the mass media or fashion, today. There might be no TV commercials so lacking in taste and charity as those for bathsoap and mouthwash. There might be no girlie magazines, no *Oh, Calcutta!* or *Without a Stitch,* no Italian "spaghetti westerns," no ugliness-for-the-sake-of-novelty in fashion designs.

I'm not saying that a good conscience will do everything for you as a parent. You'll have to do some research on your own to know how to choose the right food, discipline, and children's books for them. But what it does do, absolutely, is help you simplify. It cuts through the clutter. Clutter obscures, as any housewife knows; simplicity reveals.

Love Is All Important

According to Mary Reed Newland, "simplicity of soul is one of the prerequisites of sanctity, and it is one of the things our children already possess. . . . We must make a heroic effort to rid our lives of all but one motive, . . . a life in union with God. If this is the undercurrent of *our* existence, then we can expect the spiritual training of *our* children to bear fruit. . . . Our obligation as parents is heavy: We must raise children who are in love with God."

And how can we raise children to a spontaneous love of God, if we do not love Him and respect His rules? Dom Hubert Van Zeller writes about those who have turned a deaf ear to an "insisting voice":

"It is because the faithful have wrapped up their minds in cotton-wool that they have to be enticed, pushed, milk-canned towards good; goodness no longer appeals on its own merits. The conscience is muffled. The conscience thuds occasionally, but it doesn't jab and scream anymore. The faithful should not have to be wheedled into saying their prayers, invited to Mass and the sacraments. . . . Conscience should be doing all this, insisting with a voice which is not questioned for a moment. . . . "

When do we begin to open our children's ears to this insistent voice? How do we start to mold this exquisitely new and malleable clay? Well, I wouldn't start worrying about it the day you bring him home from the hospital. Save your energy for feeling him, keeping him dry and warm and otherwise secure in your love. For it is the expression of your love that is really the first step in clearing the site on which his conscience may grow and, hopefully, bear good fruit.

Love is more than an all-purpose sweet-smelling word which covers a multitude of ambiguous meanings. It is strong and direct, bright and warm, and, yes, it can change and hold firm your world.

Just as *charity* should not mean the check you give to keep the volunteers from your door, so too *love* should not mean that sickly affection exchanged between members of a family as exemplified in a Pillsbury cake commercial. St. Paul described the meaning of charity (love) in his letter to the Corinthians (13: 1-13). You may remember it vaguely through a Sunday sermon as a "happiness is—" exercise, but without the cuteness of the Peanuts crowd. Prod your will to go read it for yourself, and *really* read it.

Most of us have an inexhaustible lode of natural parental love to draw upon. Sometimes we overdo and overlook too much because he *is* our child. In the beginning years, we can only pray to the Holy Spirit to enlighten us so we can at least tell the difference between cuddling and coddling. A child's self-discipline (much more desirable than a parent's imposed discipline) and self-control can develop only after much hard work on the parents' part to achieve the same for themselves; and, of course,

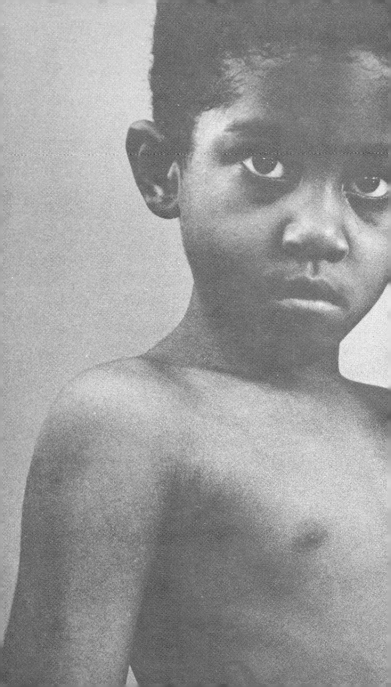

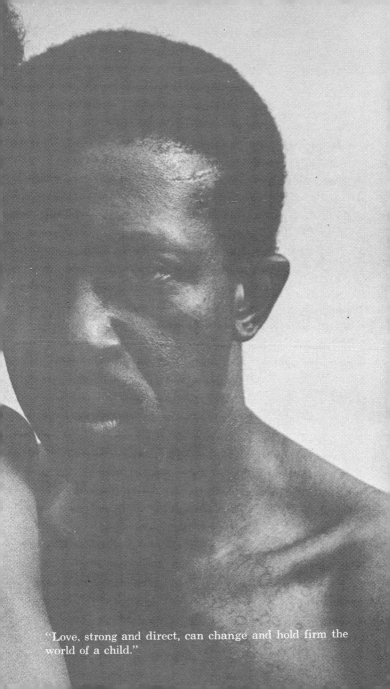

"Love, strong and direct, can change and hold firm the world of a child."

this is a continuing, ever-improving task. We must be disciplined enough to weave this spiritual design of true love into every thread of our family life. It should be done so casually, so skillfully, that the child is as unaware of it as his breathing.

In working on the growth of his conscience, I prefer to emphasize the child's desire to love and do good rather than his inclination to sin and withdraw from God. I know that the presence of sin is a serious and real experience in a child's life, and that it cannot be as lightly dismissed as the devil would tempt us to believe. But around a child, there is an aura of light, a sense of joy, in discovering everything that makes his world.

This should be heightened by encouragement instead of dampened by disapproval. Desperate resorts of "You make Baby Jesus cry when you hit Mommy," or "God is very, very angry with you for writing on the wall," and "Remember, God sees everything you are doing and will punish you," are enough to give a child a Big-Brother-is-watching-you trauma and cause more anxiety than the current episode of *Mod Squad*.

We should avoid the image of the all-wrathful, white-haired and flowing-bearded God, thundering from the heavens as He points an accusing finger at the 10-year-old smoking the stolen pack of cigarettes behind the garage. It is up to us, however, that while we dispel the illusion of God as the Ever-ready Avenger, the children don't then imagine an all-merciful God smiling down on them and patting them on the head as they puff.

Growing Up in Christ

In trying to form a God-loving rather than a God-fearing conscience, we will provide a co-coon in which the child's instinctual conscience can develop more easily into a moral one. Speaking of the stages in a child's spiritual growth, Father David O'Neill says that the child in his very early years sees right and wrong only instinctively, in relation to the parents' demands and standards. When he has a secure development of this inner control, he begins to give evidence of a loving obedience which no longer comes from a fear of consequences. This is the point, at about the ages of six to eight, which shows the first growth of what we call conscience —an awareness and true self-control in decision-making. The child detects in his parents' standards the world of reality outside the walls of his home. Actions are right and wrong in themselves, not only for him, but also for other children and grown-ups.

Then, as he is taught to pray and to understand the facts of the Gospel message, he learns about the love of God, and the love of his parents, who act as caretakers of God's property. Says Father O'Neill, "This call of God's love in the heart of the child gives an added dimension to his power of self-judgment and self-control; it opens the way to the active holiness of the Christian life, and to the possibility of committing sin. Until this added dimension grows into clear focus, a child is incapable of committing sin."

For this reason, some psychologists and theologians have stated that moral instruction emphasizing the idea of sin before this age is "psychologically harmful and theologically indefensible"—a thought which some parents have been pondering in their hearts for years!

The conclusion is that the only one who can attempt to decide whether an individual child is able to sin is someone who knows his personality and behavior very well. He must have his confidence and listen to him and bring to light his deeply personal feelings about God's love and his own behavior. Obviously this is the work of the parents.

So there we are, with our child's conscience bounced back into our responsible laps. Since we can't do much with it there, let us move it up to our intelligence and start working on a very basic framework.

Teaching the Basics

The spiritual pegs which are bedrock-basic are the Commandments, which although they have a majority of negative "Thou Shalt Nots" are ruled by the minority of two positive "Loves," which if correctly fulfilled would eliminate the negative eight. Second, there are the Beatitudes from the Sermon on the Mount, which we should know as more than peaceful pieties to be cross-stitched and hung on the wall. There is a well-ordered beauty in merely reading them; how much more so when we sincerely try to put them into effect!

Then, in small, tangible ways during the daily routine, we may introduce them to the corporal and spiritual works of mercy. This is within the possibility of all of us. None of us lead such isolated lives that we are untouched by the lonely or sick or crotchety or poor or depressed. The youngest child takes pleasure in helping bake a casserole for a family who is temporarily motherless or fixing a Christmas box for the apple man who is almost blind and lives alone with his cats (don't forget the cat food!) or wrapping a box of clothes and toys for a little girl who lives in a tenement.

At first, their satisfaction is just that of being "included in," even if it is just licking the Christmas seals or dropping the raisins in the cookie batter. It is only when he is older that he will realize that we were also helping his brother. And when you are doing these things, make sure the child knows it is in commemoration of Him, not us.

Then there is the Morning Offering which we memorized so beautifully that we could say it in 30 seconds without missing a syllable or grasping its meaning. Now that we are old and released from academic pressures, we know what it means when we offer up our prayers, works, and sufferings of this day.

This is akin to counting your spiritual chickens before they're hatched and assumes that everything you do will be for the honor and glory of God. It's certainly a positive nudge! With this attitude, we can teach them that all work, done to the best of their ability, is a prayer. Making the bed, eating oatmeal, peeling apples, searching for lizards—everything they do—can be offered up as pleasing to God.

At this age, work is still fun; they haven't yet been disillusioned by the thought that it is *work*. It is, for them, a creative expression, a source of great pride at having accomplished something that previously only grown-ups had done. They especially love to help in the kitchen. They peel and cut and grind and chatter away about such casual things as birth and death and the amazing things in between. Any mother who doesn't use this time to put in her plug for "All the way to Heaven is Heaven, etc.," is missing her big chance in her conscience-building project.

The garden is next best in lending itself to parable and parallel: the miracle of the sprouting seed, its need for water and sun to make it grow, the right soil and proper weeding, the necessity for everyone to work together so all may enjoy the harvest, the infinite variety of colors and detail which mark each growing thing —each individual, each equally beautiful.

They are amazed by the grain of a grated nutmeg, the bouquet of cauliflower "trees," the boats of pea pods, the golden smell of a pear.

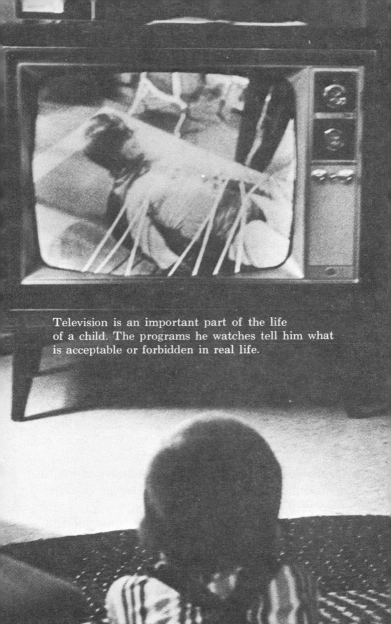

Television is an important part of the life
of a child. The programs he watches tell him what
is acceptable or forbidden in real life.

How tremendous must be the Creator of such things—and to think He made cardinals (the bird variety) and chipmunks and *babies*, too!

Family Projects

There are special incentives during Advent and Lent to keep the interest alive in offerings-up. They are, frankly, merely come-ons to taste of the Lord and see how sweet He is, but they do stir up anticipation (and sometimes competition) and give them some tangible satisfactions.

During Advent there are the straws in the manger. Each time some particularly odious deed is done (for me it's cleaning the oven) and offered up, you may put a straw in to represent your sacrifice and to help cover the floor of the stable and make it ready for the coming of the Lord. This is strictly on the honor system (no one has to reveal his deed), and I sometimes wonder if they are really keeping Christmas or just keeping up with each other.

In Lent it is navy beans dyed purple (with food coloring) which represent their good deeds. One year we used purple jelly beans. I thought this would give it an extra touch, an added incentive. I was wrong. All it did was add to the burden of temptations. Charles the Terrible, aged 3 at the time, came down late one night, or early one morning, and ate up our hard-earned sacrifices. (There was nothing in the liturgical pamphlets that could tell me how to cope with this; but then, they didn't suggest using jelly beans, either.) It wouldn't have hurt so much (us, that is) if he had developed a stomach ache, but he didn't. He was just supremely happy.

However, we "caught" his conscience at evening prayers; or rather, he caught his own. While the Morning Offering takes care of what should happen during the day, the evening examination tells us what really did. St. Francis de Sales gives us his rules for this evening practice:

"1. We give thanks to God for having preserved us during the day past.

"2. We examine how we have behaved ourselves throughout the day. . . .

"3. If we find that we have done good, we thank God for it. . . . If we have done any evil . . . we must ask pardon . . . with a resolution to confess it . . . and to make careful amendment for it.

"4. After this we recommend to Divine Providence our soul and body, the Church, our relatives, our friends. We beg our Lady and our guardian angel and all the saints to watch over us and for us. Thus with the blessing of God we go to take that rest which he has decreed needful for us."

These prayers, along the lines of St. Francis' suggestions, are brief, alive, and interesting; but then, someone else's sins are always interesting. The babies usually contribute something brilliantly wise or funny in their "Thank Yous" and

"Sorrys" (and reveal much to the parent who now knows where those chocolate cookies or roll of stamps or Martin's colored pencils have gone.)

I would not say that the humble statement, "I can't think of *anything* I did today to be sorry for" is greeted with understanding charity; there are, rather, hoots of "Get *him!*" But no matter how informal the conference seems, at least they are establishing the habit of giving thanks and submerging pride. Little acorns, drops of water, grains of sand. . . .

Most of the time we parents, mothers in particular, do not have the time for other spiritual conferences as such. We hold them impromptu in on-the-spot corrections: No, you may not hit Lucy on the head because she won't stop singing. No, you may not use Charlie's coloring book because he's in school. No, you may not pick the kitty up by the tail because you don't know where else to grab him, etc. All while you're loading the washing machine or picking up apple drops, the eternal grace, usually in the form of a question, presents itself.

The child's life is not pigeon-holed; it is one large spiritual matter in which everything relates back to God and His creativity. A book by Rachel Carson called *The Sense of Wonder* captures remarkably this sense of pristine discovery that hovers about him like a hummingbird. It is the desire to know absolutely *everything* that is the child's gift to us in helping to reach him and teach him. Where do corn flakes come from? Can you grow an egg? Who made crayons? If bees are good why do they sting us? How come Larry is black and why does his hair feel that way? How does God know how to make houses? Why is that blue jay so greedy? And on and on and on.

Every mother can fill in her own question-and-answer game. When I read of the angry frustrations of the Woman's Liberation Front over the lot of the bored, trapped housewife, I wonder whether it is more concern than lack of courage that rankles them. I wonder how any woman could be bored trying to keep up with the answers to the questions of her offspring. Trapped and frustrated, maybe, but not bored! It takes courage to stand up and be pinned down.

While it is the job of both parents to help the child be aware of what is right and wrong, it is mostly the mother who is the pattern-former of the small ones' hearts and minds—the trapped housewife. For five years or more we have them, and what they are when they enter kindergarten is the result of those mountains of minutes we have played and talked with them and fed and rocked them and secretly banged our heads on the wall with exasperation over them. Maybe not so secretly.

Day-by-Day Honesty

I think this is one of the most important arguments for mothers to stick to home base when there are little ones at home. The most valuable thing we can do is live with them, as well as love them, giving a day-by-day example for imitation. And in whatever we do, the children must see the honesty of our actions; for they have no qualms about reminding us that our actions do not match our words.

Their radar is very sensitive to phoniness. They are neither fools nor convenient Raggedy Ann dolls with which we may play and put away at our convenience. To give them the scandal of living hypocritically is a sin I'd rather not live with (if I might have a preference of sins I'd rather live with).

The search for truth by today's young adults, who take drugs to become "more aware of life's excitement" (or escape from life's mediocrity), who are triggered to demonstrate and protest and rebel against whatever does not seem just to them (however unreasoning some of the logic may seem to those of us who have been there before), may be the result of their disillusionment in the faith of their fathers and the sincerity of their mothers.

Tell the children they can't watch *Hogan's Heroes*, because concentration and P.O.W. camps were not funny, and then stand there and chuckle over them when you think they're not looking. . .

Smile at Sister Gertrude and agree with her on everything at Home School meetings and then come home and mutter about archaic old maids who care only about taking money from needy families, in front of Sister's little pupil. . .

Read to a child from the latest religious children's book, which shows how all God's children are equal in His eye, and then talk confidentially with a neighbor who drops in (the child coloring nearby) that "I'm certainly for equality but I didn't let Denise bring that little colored girl home because, well, you *know* . . . and the neighbors wouldn't understand."

Teach your child to be honest is to be free, to tell the truth always, no matter the consequences, and then let him hear you lie yourself out of working in the school cafeteria.

Tell the grocery clerk there are only 12 oranges in the bag when the child saw you put in 14 (but they were small!), or get the wrong change in your favor from a weary clerk and chuckle over it on your way home.

Lie about the origin of babies and have the child pick up some slightly different versions from school chums and it is enough to rattle his confidence and trust in his parents forever. If you are lucky, he may be charitable and merely think you dumb. To have him put his finger on you as liars is a sad thing. It may follow in his eyes that if you would not tell him what is true about birth, then you would also lie about death (maybe there is no Heaven or Hell?) and the kind of life we must lead (maybe we don't have to love God and our brother and serve them?).

It seems obvious that if we are to catch the conscience of a child, our decoy must be the real thing—the example in action of our belief

For today's young adults
decisions of conscience
involve not only
individual morality
but also a widening
sphere of
social concerns.

in Christian standards, a *single* standard. We must air out our own closets, bury forever any bothersome skeletons, put in a good bright light, keep wiping away the dust of old habits, pick off the lint of prejudice, and hang pomander balls smelling sweetly of the spice of truth.

As part of our giving good example, we must respect our children and their privacy and property as we would wish them to respect ours, and we must treat them and their behavior with as much justice as possible. When you give them a job to do, leave them alone to do it, unless they ask for help. It shows them that you have respect for their ability. Sometimes their proud work of hours may leave you grimacing. I often feel like hanging up one of those BLESS THIS MESS signs over rooms the little ones have just "cleaned." But keep this to yourself and thank them, with ceremony and diplomacy—everything short of heel-clicking and hand-kissing.

Akin to thanking them, and even more important, is apologizing to them. Very often we judge rashly or wrongly. We refuse to listen or are impatient with their demands. If our conscience is functioning smoothly, we will ask forgiveness of the child we have hurt, yes, even, a two-year-old. He holds less tightly to grudges than his parents and is extravagant with his generosity. As he is always forgiven by his parents, so he too must learn to forgive and to try to forget.

The quick temper, the rash judging, the jealousy, the puffed-up ego, the snide remark, the casual cruelty, the failure to live up to a promise or a responsibility—there is all this and more within the family. The friction of elbow-to-elbow living of age groups from infancy to middle-age rubs so abrasively you are either polished into brilliant sanctity or rubbed out completely!

So often parents feel that they have failed to reach the child who seems to reject what is good and embrace everything that is undesirable. We can only do so much (which is, everything in our power). We may instruct, admonish, suggest, give example, pray hard that we do right, but we cannot bend or break a will to our demands. We worry over our failures; what did we do wrong? Is it too late to correct it? We don't understand why God tries us so. "We see now through the mirror in an obscure manner," says St. Paul.

Yet, we all know that often within the same family, receiving the same love and instruction, there are the opposites: the good, loving, thoughtful son and the greedy, self-centered other son. They have almost become fictional stereotypes who probably had their origin in the Biblical examples of Cain and Abel and the Prodigal Son. This is part of the mystery and fascination of raising a family—we come up with such a grab bag of individuals. One will respond beautifully to the molding and grant the satisfaction of a small pride to his parents; another will reject it completely and make a parent wonder sadly how it will all end.

But we must never stop what we begin the day they are born, loving them in Christ, no matter how delightful or disagreeable they may be. After we do the best we can with the abilities we have, we must stop the spiritual nail-biting and breast-beating and leave them to God's guidance.

A good caretaker knows his limitations and when to call in the landlord.

Questions for Discussion

1. Teaching children how to love is basic for the formation of conscience. Why?

2. How can parents develop greater self-discipline in themselves so as to better help their children develop it?

3. Should a parent threaten a child that God is watching and will punish?

4. At what age do you think a child arrives at true self-control and the ability to make decisions? How do you judge this?

5. When should you introduce a child to the idea of sin? How?

6. How important do you think it is to present the Commandments positively?

7. How does the author recommend teaching the corporal and spiritual works of mercy?

8. Why does the author think that *listening* is so important for a parent in forming the conscience of a child?

9. Do you think that Advent and Lenten family practices are practical or are they forced and irrelevant? Does your family have any?

10. Is the author's plea for mothers of small children not to work justified?

11. Why is always telling the truth so important in helping a child form his conscience? Can a parent tell the truth about everything a child asks? The whole truth?

12. What does the author mean by "A good caretaker knows his limitations and when to call in the landlord"?

Chapter V

A Matter
of Conscience

Kenneth D. Eberhard, Ph.D.

One of the major conscience issues on college campuses today, at least for men, is whether they can directly participate in the Vietnam War and, if called upon, kill other human beings.

This is not, of course, a problem for all. Many young Americans judge that military service in Vietnam is their duty. They reason that the American government has been invited to South Vietnam for the legitimate purpose of helping those people maintain their freedom. If world Communism is not challenged in Southeast Asia, they argue, then it will spread and the inevitable confrontation will occur elsewhere. They understand Christ's command to love our brother as telling them to defend the South Vietnamese with the force necessary. "Greater love than this no one has," they quote the words of Christ, "that one lay down his life for his friends" (John 15, 13). We know this position. We respect the consciences of our men fighting in Vietnam.

But more and more young Americans are coming to a different decision of conscience. Do we understand and respect their reasons? We will try to explain their case.

There was a time, perhaps, when you could see it coming. He'd start skipping haircuts; the necktie would surrender to a peace medal; there'd be a march or a sit-in or a teach-in and possibly a draft-card burning. Then you'd know that Bill—your friend, brother, or son —was mulling over, perhaps even romanticizing, emigration to Canada or a prison sentence. He'd become a conscientious objector, at least to the war in Vietnam.

But sit with me in my faculty office and watch and listen to the young men as they somewhat nervously tell their stories, and you will realize that our present American image of the conscientious objector is far too narrow. Their dress, politeness and soft-spoken manner reflect a conservative family background and the conservative Jesuit university they are attending. Many have had one or two years of ROTC and received high ratings from their officers. Their parents are very proud of these young men, of that I am sure. The collegians are also sure of their parents' satisfaction, and it becomes a part of their problem: how to break it to their families that there is something in them that just won't let them put on a uniform and assist in a war that they have judged to be wrong.

A chief editor of the student newspaper told me that he knew that he couldn't answer his induction order and at the same time felt that there was no chance that his draft board would declare him a conscientious objector. Why not? Because he is not opposed to *all* wars, but feels that each war should be judged on its own basis. He's right: he doesn't qualify. And if he goes to prison, he'll have to reassess his plans for a career in public life. For not only do most states forbid ex-felons to run for public office or even vote, but there are also serious discriminations against practicing as a lawyer, doctor or teacher in a state or public school. And then, of course, any job which would require a government security clearance would simply be "not available."

This is one of the prospects for the future the collegian must consider in making his decision of conscience. It confronts my conscience also. Here are some of the most honest, courageous and idealistic young men I have ever met, and we have laws excluding them from the areas that cry out for their talent and dedication: politics, law, medicine and education.

I think of the student body vice-president who went to ROTC camp last summer and returned as a conscientious objector. "When they started to drum slogans at us like 'Marry your rifle: it's your best friend' and tell us that the reason we were there was to learn how to become killers," he told me, "I suddenly realized

Robert Bilger, right, a World War II veteran, greets his son Michael, who refused to serve in the U.S. Army.

that I personally couldn't have a part in it."

Some, I suppose, would call him a coward; others, a disloyal American. Possibly some parents might go as far as the ex-World War II fighter pilot who announced to the New York papers that his son was no longer welcome at home and that he even hoped the youth would change his name. It is even probable that there are priests and ministers who are ready to echo today the World War I statement of evangelist Billy Sunday, "The man who breaks all the rules but at last dies fighting in the trenches is better than you Godforsaken mutts who won't enlist."

The real problem of these parents and patriots, these ministers and magistrates, isn't bad will, it is difference of viewpoint. They have forgotten, or else they never learned, that both the United States and Christianity have always been sympathetic to conscientious objection and made provision for the "C.O."

A Part of U.S. Tradition

Our country's respect for the C.O. goes all the way back to 1673 when the state of Rhode Island enacted a statute in favor of anyone whose conscience would not permit him to carry arms. Nearly all of the colonies followed this practice in some form or another. New York State's original constitution in 1777 exempted Quakers from the military, and Pennsylvania exempted Moravians. When the Continental Congress met in 1774, it enacted laws in favor of religious conscientious objectors. Our draft laws of 1812 and 1863 did the same.

The reason for this is simple: many of our country's original settlers were pacifists who had been forced out of Europe. (Only a few years ago this writer was surprised to learn that his own great-grandfather came to this country because he did not want his sons to fight in the Franco-Prussian War of 1870.) Many of these people helped build our country. Of course we don't call them "draft dodgers" or "deserters" but rather "pilgrims," "immigrants," "political refugees" in search of a land where they could be free to follow their conscience.

During our Civil War, both the Confederacy and the Union, because of their desperation, became less tolerant of the conscientious objector. Nevertheless, neither side abolished the statutes, which were, in fact, more lenient than our present laws. Northerners were required to find and hire someone to take their place, while Southerners were simply assessed $500 and then absolved from their draft obligations.

When the United States officially entered World War I, it passed the national Conscription Act of 1917, which again allowed for conscientious objectors but now added some explicit restrictions. For the first time a person could qualify as an objector only if he were opposed to *all* war. Moreover, he was obliged to belong to a "well-recognized religious sect" which was opposed to war. Yet, compared to the spirit of the times, the U.S. law was still remarkably lenient. Austria, Hungary and Germany were committing all of their religious objectors to insane asylums, while France was putting its before the firing squad as deserters.

Accounts vary, but during World War II this country had between 100,000 and 170,000 of its citizens classified as conscientious objectors at one time or another. In addition, 6,000 men served prison terms for rejecting military service after being refused classification as a C.O. Twelve thousand of the recognized C.O.'s were employed in Civilian Public Service Camps, and for this they were given no pay or allowance for dependents and they were declared ineligible for the veterans' benefits given to those returning from the military.

After the war, the question of conscience took on a new importance. In the trial of the Nazi war criminals the defense argued that the accused had merely obeyed orders and therefore were not personally responsible for what had been done. This argument was rejected on the grounds that personal moral conscience comes before a patriotic blind obedience to orders. Although the command can be a mitigating factor, nevertheless, the responsibility for what one does under orders rests on the individual himself. This is the famous "Nuremberg Principle" and it reads as follows:

"The fact that the defendant acted pursuant to order of his government or of a superior shall not free him from responsibility, but may be considered in mitigation of punishment if the tribunal determines that justice so requires."

It possibly never occurred to the framers of that principle that its application would not only be made against the Nazi officials but also one day against the United States itself. Thus the recent cases of Captains Dale E. Noyd and Howard Brett Levy who disobeyed military orders because of their sense of personal and moral responsibility.

Noyd was a regular Air Force officer for 12 years, and during this time his record was impeccable. For a while he taught at the Air Force Academy in Colorado but then began to doubt the morality of the Vietnam War. He never gave his personal views in class but twice tried to resign from the Air Force. His commanding officers replied by relieving him of his Academy teaching post and reassigning him to the training of fighter pilots.

Captain Noyd petitioned for recognition as a conscientious objector and was refused because he was not opposed to *all* wars: only Vietnam. In the end, Noyd refused his order to train fighter pilots and was court-martialed and sentenced to one year's hard labor. The Jesuit weekly, *America*, commented, "Captain Noyd's trial is proof that we have not learned for ourselves the lessons we tried to teach the world at Nuremberg."

Captain Levy's case was similar. A medical officer, he was given the assignment of training Green Berets for Vietnam. According to an article in *The American Ecclesiastical Review*, when Captain Levy saw what he was supposed to teach these men, he objected on the grounds that it was contrary to International Law and to medical ethics. Invoking the Nuremberg Principle, he refused his orders. The result was a court-martial, a sentence of three years' at hard labor, and a dishonorable discharge from the Army. To careful observers it must seem that America had fallen a long way from the original ideals of her founders at the 1774 Continental Congress.

Catholic Tradition of Conscientious Objection

But if conscientious objection is a part of the American tradition, it is even more a part of the Christian tradition. Christ's Sermon on the Mount lays a scriptural basis for this when He tells us that it is the peacemakers and the persecuted whom He calls blessed. Moreover, not only does He speak against killing but even against becoming angry. This same sermon insists that when we are struck, we are to turn the other cheek. When a man demands our coat, we are to give him our cloak as well. When we are forced to walk one mile, we are to walk an additional mile. In summary, a Christian is one who loves his enemies and does good to those who hate him.

While it is well known that there are other passages in the New Testament which seem to be more tolerant towards war and violence, it is nevertheless important that the early Christian theologians did not emphasize them but embraced a pacifist position. To one who knows Church history, the list of pacifists reads like a theological *Who's Who* of the early centuries. Thus St. Clement of Alexandria (d. 215) held that Christians who became soldiers should be excommunicated. His famous disciple, Origen (d. 254), agreed, and when confronted by the philosopher Celsus with the accusation that the Christian position would lead to the downfall of the Empire, Origen had to admit that this would be so but argued that it would be a lesser evil than Christians taking up arms. The theologian, St. Justin (d. 165), advised all Christians to "scrupulously refrain" from military service. The North African theologian, Tertullian (d. 197), felt that it was against Christianity even to own a sword.

That Christians took this advice seriously we know from the story of St. Maximilian (d. 295). He was inducted into the Roman army and refused on the grounds that he was a Christian. He was cajoled and threatened but stood firm in his belief that a Christian must follow his conscience, and his conscience would not allow him to join. Maximilian was executed for his position and was soon revered by the Christian Church as a saint.

The only theologian before Constantine who seems to speak of permitting Christians to be soldiers was Hippolytus (d. 236). And he allowed them to remain in the army only if their duties did not entail the shedding of blood.

The only other exception in the early centuries to an anti-war position was the teaching of the regional Council of Arles in 314. It pronounced that the state had a right to wage war and that Christians should not throw away their weapons in time of peace.

The main tradition of pacificism was strongly expressed by the first ecumenical Church council even though the Emperor Constantine actually presided over it. The Bishops at Nicaea in 325 insisted that Christians could not voluntarily join the Roman army, and if they were forced to enter it they could never bear arms but only serve in noncombatant roles.

In that same century, St. Martin of Tours (d. 397), refused to continue as a Roman officer after his conversion; and the theologian, St. Basil the Great (d. 374), taught that any Christian who killed someone in battle should be forbidden Communion for three years as a penance.

Even in the period of the Barbarians—the Dark Ages—this tradition of conscience and war, although no longer as strong, was kept alive. In the legend of St. Gerald of Aurillac, he is described as having always fought holding his sword backwards. The legend of St. Edmund portrays him facing the Vikings alone and unarmed and being killed in the name of nonviolence. And as savage as these times were, they nevertheless had prescribed penances for killing in battle, and the clergy was always forbidden to fight.

Although the Council of Clermont (1095)

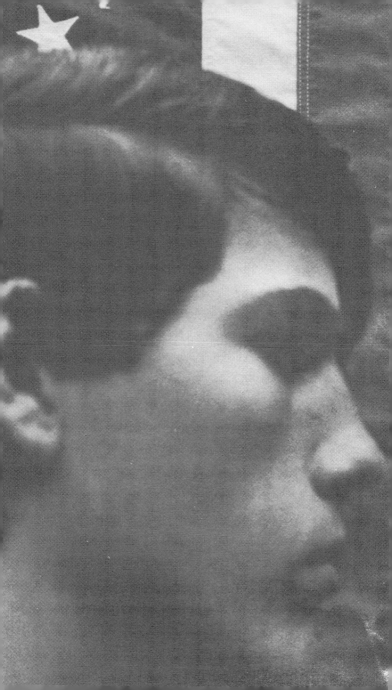

concluded with the proclaiming of the First Crusade, it nevertheless also tried to limit violence by enacting the Truce of God. This law forbade any fighting from Septuagesima to Pentecost, during Advent, and on Fridays, Sundays and holydays—thus in effect ruling out violence for over six months of every year. In the next century, the Second Lateran Council condemned the use of the crossbow as an immoral weapon, the use of which violated the Christian conscience.

Principles for Forming Conscience on War

In the 13th century, St. Thomas Aquinas in his *Summa Theologica* outlined three principles whereby a Christian was to decide whether he could participate in a particular war or not. Thomas wrote that the war must first of all be proclaimed by legitimate authority; secondly, it must be fought for a cause that is judged to be just, and thirdly, one's intention must be honorable.

In effect, this is the "just war theory" which the Catholic Church still maintains. Under this theory, some wars are considered just and some unjust. It therefore becomes a matter of Christian conscience and responsibility to decide.

The theologians today offer some further specifications of the just war theory which, in effect, place the matter even more firmly on the conscience of the individual participant. Thus they emphasize the "principle of proportionality" which says that the amount of violence used must be proportionate to the desired goal.

It is this principle which has caused some theologians to alter their opinion about the war in Vietnam. In the early stages of the conflict when there was only a limited amount of violence and hope for an early settlement, they were in favor of the war. But now the situation has changed. At this writing there have already been over 700,000 Vietnamese lives lost and three million refugees (in a country of only 36 million). Besides, 50,000 Americans have died and 300,000 have been wounded. Finally, there has been a massive destruction of the land itself. Taking all of this into account, many judge that the Vietnam War violates the principle of proportionality and is therefore unjust.

(It is pertinent to note that the great moral theologian of the 18th century, St. Alphonsus de Liguori, offered the opinion that in practice nearly all wars are immoral since they almost always escalate out of control.)

Another guide for conscience which contemporary theologians offer is the "principle of discrimination." According to this principle any war which does not discriminate between soldiers and civilians is immoral. The United States followed this principle for the greater part of the Second World War and we strongly condemned the German bombings of civilian areas at Guernica, Rotterdam and London. Our own general policy was one of daylight pinpoint bombing of

military targets even though nighttime satura-
tion bombings would have been just as effective
and at the same time have greatly reduced our
casualties. Needless to say, however, we clearly
violated the principle of discrimination at Hiro-
shima and Nagasaki, and many theologians hold
that we are continuing to violate it in Vietnam
through antipersonnel bombs and napalm.

A final principle which is added today to
explain further the theory of the just war is that
of the *ultima ratio*: the last resort. This principle
emphasizes that all other means must have been
tried and exhausted before the war can be considered just.

On this score also the conscientious objector has serious doubts about the war in Vietnam.
At the time of this writing in 1970, the "National Committee for a Political Settlement in Vietnam: Negotiation Now," points out to the
young man that our country has not tried a pro-
posal at the Paris talks that would call for 1) an
immediate cease-fire by both sides, supervised
by an international peace-keeping force; and 2)
"prompt free elections supervised by a joint
electoral commission in which all parties are
fully represented, with all sides agreeing to accept the results of the elections." If this is a rea-
sonable suggestion and if it has not yet been
proposed, then it is difficult for the objector to
see how the war can be considered as a "last
resort" and therefore just.

These principles of the just war were repeated explicitly for Catholics in the *Pastoral Con-*

stitution on the Church in the Modern World,
which was passed by an overwhelming majority
at the Second Vatican Council. There, in arti-
cles 79-82, the Council Fathers condemned the
concept of total war and "indiscriminate destruction" as well as the fact of the arms race.
They also affirmed the Nuremberg Principle
that "blind obedience cannot excuse those who
yield to (criminal actions)" and declared that
conscientious objection was a human and Christian right. Since the Council reaffirmed the just
war theory and expressed some of the criteria
under which a particular war is to be judged,
they were obviously referring not just to a conscientious objection which would extend to *all
wars* but to a *selective* conscientious objection
which would take upon itself to render a moral
judgment on each individual war.

In officially endorsing conscientious objection as a Catholic position, the Second Vatican
Council effectively countermanded a statement
by Pius XII made during his Christmas Message
of 1956. There Pius XII said:

"If, therefore, a body representative of the
people and a government—both having been
chosen by free elections—in a moment of extreme danger decides, by legitimate instruments
of internal and external policy, on defensive pre-
cautions, and carries out the plans which they
consider necessary, it does not act immorally.
Therefore, a Catholic citizen cannot invoke his
own conscience in order to refuse to serve and
fulfill those duties the law imposes."

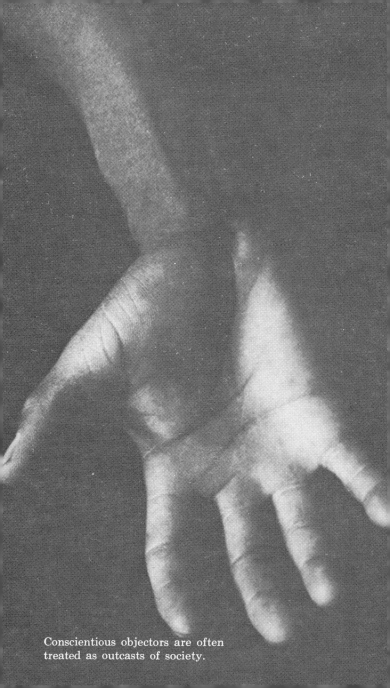

Conscientious objectors are often
treated as outcasts of society.

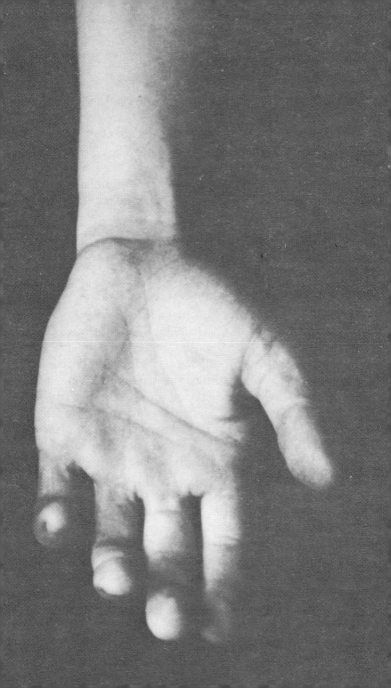

There is no doubt that many Catholics, and perhaps many draft board members, have been influenced by Pius' statement so that it was thought that one could not be a Catholic and a conscientious objector at the same time. Certainly, the Second Vatican Council is unmistakably clear when it asserts that Catholics may be C.O.'s and that governments should make provision in law for this.

Position of U.S. Bishops

In November of 1968, the American Catholic Bishops unanimously passed a statement entitled "Human Life in Our Day." If anything, the statement goes further than Vatican II in stressing the right and obligation of personal decision in conscience regarding military service. First of all, our Bishops called for an end to the draft system in the United States and the establishment of an all-volunteer army. Then, they seriously questioned whether the principle of proportionality had not been violated in the Vietnam War. They judged that many of the men who have gone to prison or suffered "social ostracism" (emigration to Canada?) have motives which "spring honestly from a principled opposition to a given war as pointless or immoral."

Further on, the document states that "frequently conscientious dissent reflects the influence of the principles which inform modern papal teaching, the Pastoral Constitution and a classical tradition of moral doctrine in the

Church, including, in fact, the norms for the moral evaluation of a theoretically just war."

In the light of these considerations, therefore, our U.S. Bishops concluded that the time has come to change our country's laws so that once again they would cover the *selective* conscientious objector and not just the man opposed to all war. In unanimously taking this stand, our Bishops not only reaffirmed a Christian tradition which dates back to the time of Christ, but they also called us to return to a tradition which is basically American as well.

Approximately one year after this historic meeting of the Bishops, the Division of World Justice and Peace of the United States Catholic Conference authored a "Statement on the Catholic Conscientious Objector." Dated October 15, 1969, it goes further than the just cited statements of Vatican II and the U.S. Bishops in drawing out some of the logical consequences of what the Church has already taught. If conscientious objection is a Christian right, then Catholics should do all that they can to support this right. It therefore recommends:

1) That each diocese initiate or cooperate in providing draft information and counseling;

2) That Catholic organizations . . . support and provide meaningful employment for the conscientious objector.

Finally, the statement urges civil officials "to consider granting amnesty to those who have suffered imprisonment and give those who have left the country an opportunity to demonstrate that they are sincerely objectors."

This same plea for amnesty was repeated by the well-known and respected Archbishop of Boston, Cardinal Cushing, in his 1970 Easter Message. Commenting favorably on this position, *Commonweal* estimated that the amnesty would pertain to about 100 in the Allenwood Prison, 15,000 Americans living in Canada, 500 throughout Europe and about another 1,200 elsewhere in the United States.

That a young man can find grounds for conscientious objection is clear to me. Some may still object by arguing that no individual ever has enough evidence to pass judgment against his country's war or military orders. But this is to demand a false kind of certitude and basically is the same argument used to defend the Nazi officials at Nuremberg. No one is ever completely certain about political matters. Instead, we make the best informed judgment that we can and assume a personal responsibility for it.

One can never hand his conscience over to his government, and it is only the simpleminded who automatically equate a prison sentence with a disrespect for the laws of the land. As Martin Luther King pointed out in his famous *Letter from Birmingham City Jail*, it can be an act of *highest* respect for the law if one goes to prison in order to call attention to laws which are unjust.

And so I agonize with the young men whose first words to me are, "I don't know if I'm go-

ing to prison or to Canada, but I do know that I'm not going to fight in Vietnam. Can you help me?" Their parents will probably react with something like, "Tom, why do you have to go upsetting everyone like this? Think of your future."

Yes, Tom, why do you have to upset everyone? Why do you have to upset *me*? I'd rather read my books and teach my classes and be left alone. So would 50 million other American Catholics . . . and that's the *real* problem.

Questions for Discussion

1. How would you describe a conscientious objector? What is the popular American image of the C.O.?
2. The conscientious objector is sometimes confronted with the spoken or unspoken charge: "Any red-blooded, really patriotic American is happy to fight for his country." What response could be made in defense of the C.O.?
3. What is the present attitude of the Church regarding *selective* conscientious objection?
4. When was the restriction added to U.S. law that to be classified as a conscientious objector one had to be opposed to *all* war?
5. Would you favor federal legislation to protect the *selective* conscientious objector?
6. In the first three centuries of Christianity what did theologians teach regarding Christians taking part in wars?
7. How does one decide on whether a war is just? What do theologians mean by the principle of proportionality in regard to war? The principle of discrimination? The principle of the last resort?
8. How far can parents go in helping their children form their consciences on the morality of a war?

An Afterword

to answer two common objections

I hate priests who say, "I don't know."

Probably it is true that some of us priests dodge hard questions. Also, after years of urging the laity to depend on priestly advice, maybe we are expecting too much maturity of conscience too quickly. But try to look at the current scene through the priest's eyes.

First, there are a lot of things the priest *does* know and does proclaim emphatically without hesitancy day in and day out: the generosity that God's love demands of us, the need to worship God, to love our neighbor, to give every man his just due, to respect our own bodies as well as the bodies of others, to pray. Do you really want him to spell out all the applications? Do you want him to preach on how he has made up his conscience on the morality of the Vietnam war? Shall he decide whether you should move out of a changing neighborhood? How many children you should have?

Second, some laymen seek to maintain an unhealthy dependence on a priest to give them all the answers and take all the responsibility. The priest may refuse to give you an answer because he doesn't want "to take you off the hook." He wants you to assume responsibility for your moral decisions. The priest can help you understand the meaning of the Gospel, he can tell you what the laws are and give you advice as to their application, he can assist you in honestly and sincerely studying the facts. You have to make the decision and live by it.

Finally, maybe we've built up some false expectations. We should not imagine that the Scriptures contain answers to all the specific problems of 20th-century living. The Bible gives us insights and values but not specific answers to problems unforeseen centuries ago. Christ promised to tell us what we need to get to heaven. He didn't say He would solve all problems and dissipate all doubts.

So, maybe the priest (or the Church) really doesn't know the answer. Perhaps it is your task as a layman to search for it. This is the suggestion of the *Church in the Modern World*. "Laymen should also know that it is generally the function of their well-informed Christian conscience to see that the divine law is inscribed in the life of the earthly city. From priests they may look for spiritual light and nourishment. Let the layman not imagine that his pastors are always such experts, that to every problem which arises, however complicated, they can readily give him a concrete solution, or even that such is their mission. Rather, enlightened by Christian wisdom and giving close attention to the teaching authority of the Church, let the layman take on his own distinctive role" (43).

It's not within a priest's power to make all decisions easy and simple with guaranteed results. Maybe once we thought it was. Now all of us are more realistic.

Isn't this stressing the role of conscience going

to lead to laxity? Aren't a lot of people going to get away with doing just what they want?

That's possible. If they do, it is "on" their conscience. We cannot deny the human tendency to justify as moral whatever we want to do. Our wish becomes father to our thought, as Shakespeare says. If what we are doing is at variance with our way of thinking, we change either one or the other.

But trying to have every obligation spelled out in detail so that there is little for the individual to decide for himself also has its risks. Because of past attempts to do this, we now have an overabundance of inactive consciences. Such dormant consciences are moved to act only when commanded by law. They cannot understand the poverty of the Third World or something like open housing as a moral issue. "There's no law saying that anybody has to live next to a Negro."

Besides, no one can put down directives to cover everyone in every situation in our complex world.

Actually, an active conscience, as promoted in this book, will lead not to laxity but to generosity.

The active conscience should keep everyone from just "doing his own thing" because each of us is confronted with the same basic realities. The most basic of these is God's love for us and His insistence that we love one another and grow in awareness of and response to communal, social, cosmic obligations. The Commandments give some direction how we do this. The same word of God is proclaimed to all Christians from the Bible. The same Spirit breathes within us. The same Church speaks to all Catholics on the application of the Gospels to our faith and living today.

Conscience has to face *all* of reality. It is not so much the originator of its own principles and guidelines and criteria for decision. It must learn them. It must then apply and express in living human action what it has learned. The Christian seeks in faith to be aware of God, the world, society, himself. In light of this he seeks to discern and decide how to act responsibly, in a way that will be pleasing to God and promote the good of self and others.

In this book conscience has been explained as the response to love. Precisely what is the loving thing to do is sometimes not easy to decide. One thing is sure, love can never give enough. It is always eager to see how it can do more. Don't we often say that we do things for love that we would never do for money or any other reason? What can ask more from us than love? —Jeremy Harrington, O.F.M.

About the Authors

Cyrin Maus, O.F.M., S.T.D., earned his doctorate at the *Antonianum* in Rome and has since taught dogmatic theology at St. Leonard College in Dayton, Ohio. From 1967 to 1970 he also served as president of the college. In 1966 he participated in the International Congress of Theology of Vatican II in Rome.

Nicholas Lohkamp, O.F.M., S.T.D., received his doctorate in moral theology from the Catholic University of America in 1956 and has since done further study at the University of San Francisco and Boston University. He taught for two years at St. Francis College in Fort Wayne, Indiana, and for 12 at St. Leonard College Dayton, where he was also director of formation. Presently he is academic dean there, professor of moral theology, and also serves as chaplain to the Dayton Catholic Physicans Guild.

Ethel Marbach as the mother of five daughters and three sons speaks from experience in "To Catch the Conscience of a Child." Providing for her husband, a college professor of English, and her children near Moscow, Pa., has given her material for two books, *A Do-It-Yourself Guide to Holy Housewifery* and the *Holy Housewifery Cookbook*.

Kenneth D. Eberhard, Ph. D., earned his master's in theology at the University of San Francisco and his doctorate at Graduate Theological Union, Berkeley. He has also done further study in Belgium and Germany. Presently he is assistant professor of theology at Xavier University, Cincinnati, and serves as part-time draft counselor. He is married and has a daughter.

PHOTO CREDITS